The Success Theory Handbook

The Success Theory Handbook

DO LIFE A BETTER WAY...YOUR WAY!

Mario Porreca

ISBN: 0692867090
ISBN 13: 9780692867099
Library of Congress Control Number: 2017904752
Badass Press, Belle Vernon, PA

To human beings: We are all beautiful, we are all amazing, and we all deserve to be successful in our own special ways. Here's to chasing, creating, and living your own vision of success while helping others do the same.

Contents

Foreword

"**Y**ou have two options. Change or don't."

I remember the first time Mario said those words to me. All I could think was, "You gotta be f——— kidding me." With all the endless possibilities in this vast world of ours, how could there be only two choices?

As we talked—or rather as Mario talked and I listened—it dawned on me that as humans, we make things so darn complicated, but it doesn't have to be that way.

Like all things in life, success really can be simple. It's just not easy, but the way the success theory is broken down in this book certainly proves that it is, in fact, simple.

I tend to complicate things—like writing this foreword. I first wrote a big, elaborate story about the events that led me to this place and was so far off the map of tying it back to whatever the heck the point was that I didn't even know what point I was supposed to make in the first place, and I was writing the darn thing! So yes, I would definitely say I am good at complicating things, but my alter ego says maybe I just like a good challenge.

Now, it's one thing to complicate a simple task or project, but it's quite another to live an entirely complicated life. I know because my life used to be so complicated. Imagine trying to be something you're not every waking moment of every day for months on end—that's what "complicated" looks and feels like.

Looking in from the outside, almost everyone thought I had a great life—I had a great-paying job in marketing, owned a beautiful townhome filled with pretty things, was married, drove a brand-new car, went shopping when I wanted-ed, and took fun vacations multiple times a year—but my truth was I could not have felt more miserable, trapped, and unfulfilled in nearly every aspect of my life.

I always wondered what rock bottom would feel like for me—I found out firsthand during a bender in Vegas. The crash was painful in every way, and I finally had no choice but to face my situation with brutal honesty.

At the bottom, my protective bubble I thought I was fooling people with had burst. All my dysfunctional, sabotaging behaviors were fully exposed. I realized how far off course I was and that my life choices were simply not sustainable anymore.

Hitting rock bottom was the beginning of questioning everything I ever thought to be true. I questioned my motives, other people's motives, my beliefs, my fears, why I did things, why I didn't do things, why I attracted certain people and circumstances, why I succeeded, and why I failed. The very fabric of my life was turned upside down and examined in raw and emotional detail by a therapist twice a week. I began to look at things with a fresh perspective based on a renewed sense of clarity.

What I learned from all of it is this:

1. You don't really know it's rock bottom until you begin to climb out.
2. It gets worse through growth so it can eventually get better.
3. Don't make your rock bottom lower than it has to be.

Owing to this experience, I made the choice to let go of everything, because nothing was working.

So by the time I met Mario, to say I was in a transition is an understatement—I had sold my house, had quit my job, was traveling the country with my dog and a pending divorce in tow, and was in full badass-babe mode on the adventure of a lifetime.

We spent hours talking on the phone, getting to know each other. The more miles I drove, the more I verbally processed the aftermath of my major life changes and all the what-ifs. We talked about questions like, What do I want to do with my life once my road trip is over, and how do I make money without going back to exactly what I was doing? We also talked about daily small challenges, like, Where am I going to sleep, where can I use the bathroom at two in the morning, and when and where I can take a shower next?

Mario helped me connect the dots and really dig deep into what I would think was the simplest of comments but was more telling as to where my head was in the process of changing.

At the time I thought it was all just casual conversation, but after reading this book, a light bulb went off! There was a true method to the madness, and I was really the first graduate of the success theory! I can tell you from a place of real-world experience that this works, because I have lived the success theory firsthand through working with Mario.

Before I applied the success theory, I thought I would move back to Chicago, get an apartment in River North with some friends, continue to build a real estate–rehab empire, and settle into a new normal.

However, I was still on a major change trajectory. The principles of the success theory were driving me toward discovering my great purpose, which led me to Pittsburgh, the creation of our lifestyle brand, Badass Life, and this very book.

I not only believe in these principles; I live and breathe them, and I am so thankful for where this process has guided me, solidifying my purpose to share this theory with others and pay it forward. Now, Mario and I get to spend every day teaching the success theory and helping others unlock their true purposes.

I invite you to get comfy before diving into learning about what has made such a profound impact in our lives and the lives of so many people Mario and I have the pleasure and opportunity of working with. Also, visit us at TheSuccessTheory.com for more info and resources and to get to know us better. We're always eager to help, share, grow, learn, and contribute. We all know it's not real unless it's Facebook official, so be sure to connect with us there too at Facebook.com/BadassLife.

Enjoy the success theory, and we'll be here, living our mission to help you do life a better way…YOUR way!

Smooches!
Erica Parr
Pittsburgh, Pennsylvania
March 2017

First Things First

I was staring at a blank whiteboard with a dry-erase marker in my hand. As superheroes stare down the villain with their weapons in hand, so was I in the same situation with the same feeling—while wearing tights and a cape.

Maybe that last part was a bit embellished, but I have an active imagination I like to employ pretty much all the time to keep life fun. The truth is I was staring down the four whiteboards that hang on our apartment wall. I was staring at them with a green marker in my right hand, a pile of various colored markers on the table next to me, and so many ideas flowing through my head it reminded me of a river flowing madly toward a waterfall.

I was standing there staring, trying to get myself to figuratively leap into the river of chaos and safely ride the rapids over the falls to the oasis that awaited below. This clever metaphor is all a way of saying I could feel the ideas and impact inside of me, I was yearning to get it out in a way in which I could use it to contribute to and serve others, and it had to allow me to grow as a person and a leader at the same time.

I took a deep breath and a sip of black tea, but not at the same time, and then pressed the marker to the board with the intention of seeing and organizing my ideas in the hopes of deciphering the path to this magical destination in true Tom Hanks / Nicholas Cage movie-character style.

The marker darted across the board, and what transpired over the course of the next few hours looked like a complete mess—a completely beautiful mess that I stepped back and smiled at proudly, complete with goose bumps. It was chaos, but it was, as one of my mentors taught me in my professional-chef days, controlled chaos. Chaos by itself is messy and ugly, but control the chaos, and it becomes a beautiful choreographed dance capable of creating results of epic proportions!

This guide is the result of that controlled chaos, which all began with the first thing birthed from that green dry-erase marker. Little did I know when I began writing how impactful the first board of information would end up being. It was nothing magical and really wasn't deep-level stuff, but it was a starting point, and it was made up of four critical questions I find myself coming back to time and time again.

Those questions are so critical and that board was so beautiful that now, looking back, I'd like to present it to you first in all its glory. Take a good long look at those questions and how they flow, and just think about them. Starting the handbook this way might not make a lot of sense at the moment, but there is a strategic reason we are doing this.

This handbook is made up of four key sections, and each section explains a key component of the success theory. Each section is immediately followed by key questions built from those components. Those questions build upon one another and are designed for you to put some thought into and answer so you have a path to follow to creating your version of success.

I firmly believe we already have everything we need within us to become successful. You are enough—you know enough, you care enough, you believe enough, and you are capable of taking enough action RIGHT NOW to reach a higher level of your own success. The key is to learn more, care more, believe more, and take more action as you travel along on your own journey.

Most of us who are very driven, ambitious, and success oriented spend too much time consuming content and "getting ready" to become successful. I am guilty of falling into this trap as much as anyone. I mean, come on. It's fun to learn new things, and it's exciting to become motivated and grow our internal levels of inspiration.

Execution, on the other hand, usually is fun only at first. It's fun when you start and things are new, fresh, and exciting! But then some time goes by, and if you're too focused on executing and not so much on growing, you can contribute only so much, and a plateau inevitably hits. Plateaus suck—that's really the nicest way of putting it. **The key is to execute consistently at a high level while simultaneously continuing to learn, grow, and develop so you always have more value to share and contribute to others.**

Tony Robbins is one of my idols and mentors, and he teaches that all human beings have six basic needs. You can Google them and let Tony teach you all about the six needs, as he is the master and you will undoubtedly get the most value from learning about them directly from the source.

That said, I do want to touch on the fact that Tony teaches that the last two human needs of the six are what he calls the needs of the spirit, and those are growth and contribution. Tony teaches that we all meet the first four needs, which he calls the needs of the personality, in either a constructive or destructive way, but we all meet those needs 100 percent of the time. The needs of the spirit, though, are the needs that create fulfillment and therefore, in my mind, are the most crucial to focus on.

As long as we meet our needs for certainty, variety, significance, and love/connection in constructive ways, we can then place a majority of our conscious focus on growing as human beings and using that growth to contribute to others beyond ourselves in a positive way—and that, my friends, is the secret that will lead you to true fulfillment.

The good news is you already have what you need to start doing this right now, this very second. The confusing news is you may not yet know where or how to get started. The best news is you have this handbook to use to begin guiding yourself on the path to where you want to be. I say "guiding yourself" because this book doesn't contain the answers—it contains the questions, and you contain the answers. This handbook will help you unlock your own mind and your own desires and help you get into action to start making those desires a reality.

Once you work through this handbook and want more continued support, then rest assured we have you covered! We have ongoing content and options to work with us one-on-one; you can join our Stir the Pot Mastermind Group, link into our community, and more. The only reason I mention all these options right off the bat is because I want you to know there are always more opportunities available.

My mentors and the groups I associate with are invaluable to me and are constantly assisting me to level up on my journey. My mission is to pay it forward and help others do the same—I want you to level up so you can pay it forward and contribute more to others. Growth isn't just something that makes you better and gives you more tools and success; it's also an obligation for you to contribute value to others. It's serious, and it's the true embodiment of personal fulfillment.

So are you still curious as to what was on that very first dry-erase board? It was like the first snowflake that built the snowman that led to joy for all the children. I'm going to share it with you as promised, and then, in the first section of this handbook, we are going to dive into redefining success so you know exactly what true success looks like to you personally. It's much easier to achieve something when you know what it looks and feels like at an emotional level. I am also going to break down and explain the success theory in detail, AND I'll show you how you can look at any successful person and reverse engineer his or her success using it.

Thinking and brainstorming is a unique process that, if practiced and done intentionally, allows us to tap into intelligence far greater than our own. I believe inspired thoughts and ideas come from somewhere far greater than us. I believe we are all here for a specific reason and if we are persistent enough to find that reason so we can execute on it and accomplish the things we are here for, we will get some much-needed help. We typically called this help "inspired" or "inspiration" or "miracles," or we say things like "It just came to me" or we had a "gut feeling." The key is that we have to have a strong desire, be persistent, and be open to possibilities far greater than we can fathom. When we are operating with this energy at that wavelength, then "miracles" happen.

The things I come up with and the ideas I have the honor of sharing aren't my own. They come from me, but they are inspired by something far greater. I learned a long time ago while going through this process and searching for my own purpose that I had to let go and become the instrument, so to speak. When we take ourselves out of the equation, we become so much more powerful because power is in serving others. The most powerful people are the people who operate out of the desire purely to serve others with no expectations of anything in return. When we are tied to expectations, we aren't really serving others; we are serving ourselves. And if we are really serving only one person, how can we make the world a better place? Pure contribution to as many people as possible is the key to fulfillment, as stated many times above.

Are you excited?

Are you ready to dive in?

Here's how it all began and in my opinion the best place to begin—with these questions in this order:

**What are you good at?
What do you love doing?**

**Why do
you care?**

**How do you
get paid to do
that?**

SECTION I

Redefining Success

T he dictionary tells us that success is "the accomplishment of an aim or purpose." I'm not saying the dictionary in all its wordy wisdom is wrong, but I'm not willing to say it's correct in this case either.

Success is such a personal thing, and what it looks and feels like specifically is different for everyone. For some people, success looks like fame and riches, for others it looks like a promotion at work, and for others it looks like getting to spend more time with family or going on an extra vacation. It all depends on your personal dreams and how you want your life to look and feel. There is no right way or wrong way; there is just your own way.

Many people fall into the trap of associating money and significance with success, and maybe that's what you personally desire—but success in and of itself is so much more than that. I know some people who have more money than they could spend in five lifetimes, and they are still miserable. Meanwhile, I know others who have enough money to sustain their lifestyles and maybe a bit extra at most and are extremely happy and driven in their lives. They are making a difference, have a purpose, and are fulfilled as they pursue every day as a brand-new opportunity to give more to the world. It's all a matter of perspective.

You will NEVER achieve success if you don't know what success looks and feels like for you. Think about it—if you want to go to, say, Walt Disney World, you have a much better chance of actually meeting Mickey if you know where on the planet Disney World is located and if you know what it looks like when you arrive. But wait one minute; let's back up this train, as I seem to have gotten ahead of myself.

Before you even go to Google (I almost said "grab a map," but who even uses those anymore?) and search for Disney World and learn where it's located and what it looks like, you have to have an idea of why you want to go there in the first place. You don't go to Disney World to see a castle, meet characters from movies come to life, or even ride amazing and fun amusement park rides—you go to Disney World for a feeling! You go there to feel the way the way you feel when you're there. Some people describe it as fun, others as nostalgic, and others even commonly describe it as "magical." You search for Disney World and eventually make your way there because of either the feeling that being at Disney World creates for you OR the feeling that seeing your family having a magical experience at Disney World creates for you.

Once you discover this feeling you want to have, you begin the process of figuring out where it's located, how you get there, and what it's going to cost you in terms of both time and money to get there and be able to experience this feeling. The reason so many people spend a lot of time and money to go on a Disney vacation or cruise is because the magical feelings it creates are worth more to them than the time and money they have to trade to make the experience happen.

Everything we do and pursue as human beings we do to achieve a feeling. If you've ever wanted a specific type of car or house or even wanted to be live in person at the Super Bowl or Disney World, it's all because of the feeling you were going to have. That feeling of sitting behind the wheel of your absolute dream car or in the living room of your dream house or in the stands with the massive crowd while the entire world watches from their homes or holding your little princess while her eyes light up at seeing Cinderella's castle in person for the very first time—it's all for the feeling.

That feeling is the most important part of the process because the feeling drives everything. The good news is you can actually give yourself permission to feel that same exact feeling whenever you want. You can close your eyes right now and feel any of the feelings I described above, if they are applicable to your life. In fact, I recommend to people I work with that they regularly spend time each day not only dreaming about the things they wish to accomplish but actively feeling the feelings they want to create in real life. I recommend feeling them completely and visualizing every single detail of the experience, from the smells in the air at the Super Bowl to the crown your little princess is wearing outside of Cinderella's castle. It's all in the details and making the feeling as real and as strong as possible. That feeling is the driving force behind accomplishment and also the reward for accomplishing it.

What I'm getting at with all the examples and visualizations is that success isn't easy. It takes real work, and it takes overcoming real obstacles. This is a good thing because nothing worthwhile comes easy. However, when you make the commitment to level up and create your version of success in your life, you better go there in your mind first and experience it as often as possible to keep reminding yourself how much it is worth to you. Visualization and feeling the feelings create desire and urgency. Strong desire coupled with urgency mixed with persistence is an unbeatable recipe.

The questions following this section will help you begin to define, identify, uncover, and visualize what success in your life looks like. You will then begin to develop a strategic plan for creating this success so you get to experience in real life all the fantastic feelings you're going to create in your mind.

Before we get into specifics, let's talk about the success theory itself. Now that you are reframing success and identifying it according to yourself, we can get more into the specific steps every single successful person since the beginning of time has taken. The success theory is a working theory I developed and continue to prove over and over again by identifying specific steps/actions successful people have taken and people who are pursuing success are taking.

If you start with your end goal in mind, you can reverse engineer it using the success theory to create the results and feelings you desire. The following sections of this handbook will each cover one aspect of the success theory and walk you through using it to create a strategic plan for accomplishing your version of success in your own life.

The success theory is composed of three parts. It's really not anything magical, mysterious, or amazing—it's simply a set of steps I have identified from talking to and working with a lot of different people who are either successful already or on their way.

Let's put the success theory to the test right off the bat. Think of someone in your life whom you would consider successful in some endeavor, or think of a specific area of your own life where you consider yourself quite successful. On a piece of paper, write down that person's name and the area in which you consider him or her successful. As soon as I reveal the success theory to you, list the ways in which this person's (or your own) success came from the specific steps included. Ready? Let's do this. Ladies and gentlemen, I present to you the following:

PURPOSE + MASTERY + SERVICE = SUCCESS

1. Purpose: Find something you both love and are good at.
2. Mastery: Practice and constantly improve to become the best you possibly can be in your area.
3. Service: Use this skill to serve and positively impact as many people as possible.

It seems simple, and it is simple—success is simple. However, it's anything but easy. Each of the three steps that make up the success theory poses its own unique challenges; however, it's much easier to accomplish success when you first know what success looks and feels like to you, use that to drive and motivate you, and then have a working map in the form of the above steps to follow.

This handbook will assist you in breaking down and following the success theory in your own life to create the success you desire. That said, realize that while I can help you—and it is my own quest and purpose to help others achieve their dreams—I can help you only as much as you help yourself. You have to dig deep to create the look and feel of success in your own life. If you think you've uncovered it but still find yourself not completely driven to go above and beyond and do whatever it takes to make it happen, you have to go back to your own whiteboard to redesign and start over.

Once you uncover your true purpose and begin the process of mastering it, you'll know it. I can't explain how or why or even what you will experience, but it will be unlike any endeavor you've set out to achieve. You won't be able to stop the mastery process. That last sentence is the real key—anytime we quit or give up on anything, it's because we give up or quit on ourselves. Others may feed into the process and even expedite it a bit, but when you find your true purpose, nothing will be able to stop you. You might walk away for a moment or two, but you'll be back, and you'll keep coming back time and time again. So my question becomes, why fight it?

Begin the search for your purpose now by experiencing and trying new things. Dive into life, and see what you come out with. Deep down inside, we all know why we are here and we all know what our purposes are. Typically, if you think back to your childhood as early as you can remember, you most likely did something or were interested in something that just came naturally to you. It was something you were both good at and loved doing, and you just did it because you didn't know any better. The "real" world had yet to teach you your own limitations—which are all completely self-inflicted, by the way.

Go back to being that curious, carefree child you once were, and explore the things you loved to do before you were told to be "realistic." Now, I'm not saying all of us as children did something intuitively we were meant to pursue the rest of our lives. I am saying that typically, if you look back with a newly opened mind, you will uncover some clues you forgot about or didn't see before that can lead you to an aha moment.

For me personally, I always liked to entertain people. I remember when I just learned to walk and talk, I would sneak into my dad's chiropractic office, which was connected to our home, and I would sing, dance, and act out complete scenes from *The Wizard of Oz*, *Willy Wonka*, and *Dumbo*. I would watch the movies over and over and over again and memorize certain scenes, and I would even gather clothes and toys as costumes and props. I loved being in front of a group of people, and I loved to entertain them.

I'm pretty certain I'm never going to be a great actor, at least not one who gets paid. However, I do still love public speaking, and I love to have an impact on people's lives in a positive way and see them get excited, become happy, and create results for themselves. I couldn't do that as a young child, but I could get in front of people and make them smile and laugh through my attempt at acting. I didn't have the material back then, but I began the mastery process because it was something that just came naturally to me and was an intuitive behavior. I can look back throughout the years and see where I would intuitively try to get in front of people to entertain and teach them in different ways. Even though I may have succumbed to the world and given up on my acting dreams, I still continued and continue to come back for more time and time again because I know my purpose is to help as many people as possible take control of their lives and to do it in a fun, interactive, and entertaining way.

You don't have to be amazing to make a profound impact. Whenever I stop in to see my dad at his chiropractic office, there are people who tell me they remember when I would entertain them as Willy Wonka all those years ago. I was a child and didn't have a plan; I just did what came naturally, and I made an impact. Can you imagine the profound impact you can make on others as an adult with a real plan?

So let's get intentional and start to build your plan and put it into action. Let's work on uncovering your own look and feel of success and identifying and describing it in as much detail as possible. If you're anything like me, you probably aren't into answering the questions that books give you. You just want to read and consume the content and see what you learn and move on. Though I was guilty of that in the past, I don't do it anymore, because through uncovering the success theory, I take full responsibility for my life and the results I create. I can consume all the material in the world, but if I don't do the work myself and put what I learn into action immediately, I can never expect to create the results I want to create in my own life. We all have to do our own work in our own lives, and until we are ready to accept that responsibility and step up to the plate, nothing is going to change. I'm sure you've heard the saying "Nothing changes if nothing changes." So change something and spend some serious time and thought on the questions that follow each section of this book. You are creating your own version of success in your life, and if you don't actively work to create it, nobody else is going to. Get excited, tackle these questions, and then bring them with you to the next section in this handbook, which is all about talent and purpose.

THE SUCCESS THEORY HANDBOOK

Creating Your Success

A. What does success look like to you?
B. What are three specific areas of your life where you consider yourself successful?
C. Where would you like to create more success in your life, and what does that look like? Be as descriptive as possible.
D. Who is the most successful person you know personally, and what are three questions you would like to ask this person about his or her success?
E. If you could wake up tomorrow and live as if time and money were no issue in your life, in detail, what exactly would your day look like?

SECTION II

Talent and Purpose

"**B**e realistic." I'm sure you've heard that phrase before. In my personal experience, that phrase is something unhappy or unfulfilled people use to try to make the rest of us feel as close to how they feel as possible. The phrase implies we should do something "real" or, more specifically, "real easy." Be realistic, don't get your hopes up, just do what you have to do, it is what it is—I especially despise that last one.

Just writing that previous paragraph puts me in a bit of a funk. How did reading it make you feel? That's a serious question; it was a bit of a pop quiz, if you will. I want you to see where you stand as far as the stories you tell yourself and, more specifically, the stories you've been telling yourself for so long you now believe them to be true.

The truth is we were all born with zero beliefs. We had no opinions, no beliefs, no ideas, and no stories. We were happy. When we were born, we came into the world with two natural fears that are innate in all of us, and we also arrived with a natural curiosity about these new people we were suddenly sharing a room with and this new world we were suddenly a part of. The two natural fears, by the way, that we are all born with are the fear of loud noises and the fear of falling. Aside from that, everything else we pick up along the way is learned. The good news is if it can be learned, it can also be unlearned if it's not serving you.

Well, there are at least two other things we are born with that I failed to mention, and I believe these things come from our creator. These things are, of course, our talents and our purpose, and if we are creative enough, we can use one in some form or fashion to accomplish the other.

Before we go ahead and tie the two together, let's focus on what a talent really is. I mean, we've all been taught since we can remember that every person has a unique talent or even set of talents. We are also taught that our talents are certain things we have just been blessed with and are naturally good at. While this is generally true, I believe it goes deeper than that.

The level and the manner in which we choose to master our talents and then share them with the world is the variable and the thing that separates someone who is talented with a paintbrush from a true artist. We have these things that are natural gifts and they are absolutely a blessing we possess and have been gifted; however, it then becomes our responsibility to figure out what these talents are, how to further develop and master them, and finally how to use them to serve as many people as possible in a positive and profound way. When I say "profound," I don't mean it has to be earth shattering, but I do mean our talents should serve others beyond ourselves and make the world a better place for that person or group of people. You don't have to change the world for everyone, but sometimes changing the world for one person creates a ripple effect that changes everything. You never know where it will go and where it will end up when you do something good for someone else.

I don't know what your talent is, but I do know you have one. **It's up to you to figure out what you are good at, tie that skill into something you love doing, and then master whatever that becomes while using it to serve as many people as possible.** Read that last sentence again. In fact, read it a few times—because that is your purpose.

So many people get hung up on what they are placed on this planet to do, and they go on these huge quests to try to figure it out. Sometimes these journeys take years, and by the time they come to any sort of valuable conclusion, they've cut the time they could be contributing their gifts to the world in half. The question to ask yourself isn't, what is my purpose? There are actually three questions you need to ask yourself if achieving your personal vision of success is important to you—and it should be, because the greatest way you can serve the world is to become successful yourself. Reaching your personal vision of success will not only allow you to serve as many people as possible while utilizing your natural gifts and abilities, but it will also provide a shining example of what is possible and "realistic" to others. Success is your responsibility; it's all of our responsibility.

So what are the four questions you need to ask yourself to uncover your true purpose?

1. **What do I love to do?**
2. **What am I naturally good at?**
3. **How can I combine these things in a manner that will serve others?**
4. **How can I use this to serve as many people as possible and get paid to do that?**

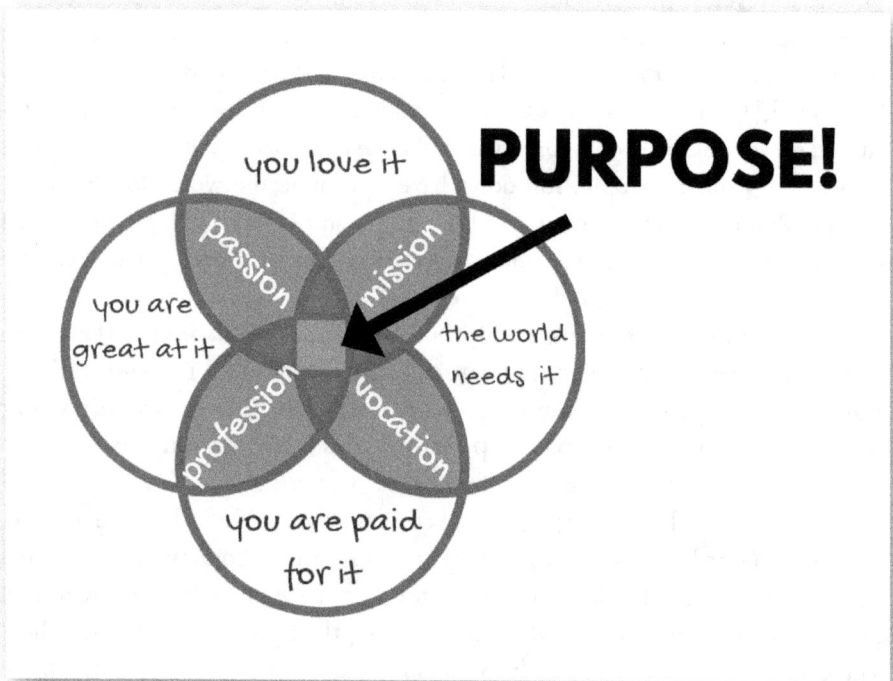

One question leads into the next, and once you completely work through them, you will come to a conclusion that serves both you and others while leveraging and utilizing what you're naturally good at and love to do while also considering how you can be compensated financially for doing that. The questions are very simple, and the process is very simple, but it's not an easy process. It takes a lot of self-reflection, thought, emotion, honesty, and desire to answer each of these questions. Even so, the Good Book tells us a very important law

when it comes to self-discovery, especially when your intentions are pure—
"Seek and ye shall find." It doesn't say it will be a fast or even an easy process,
but it does promise that if the desire is there and you are persistent, you will be
successful and find what you are searching for.

When it comes to the above purpose questions, it is vital that what you
discover is a skill, task, or mission you *both* love and are good at, and there a
couple of reasons for this. First, you must love it because you are going to have
to devote a lot of time to it. Whether practicing, learning, or executing whatever
it is, you're going to have to further develop it, and it's not going to be easy all
the time. If you don't love what it is you are doing, the hard times will seem even
harder, and giving up at some point is inevitable.

We all go through a natural cycle of growth that further emphasizes how
vitally important it is to love the skill, task, or mission you choose to pursue
and master. The cycle of growth is made up of four phases everyone who starts
something new goes through. The time each person spends in each phase of
the cycle varies with a number of factors, but if you can recognize the different
phases, you'll be able to not only see which phase you are currently in but also
prepare for the phase that's coming. Anticipation and preparation are both extremely valuable skills to practice effectively. The cycle of growth looks like this:

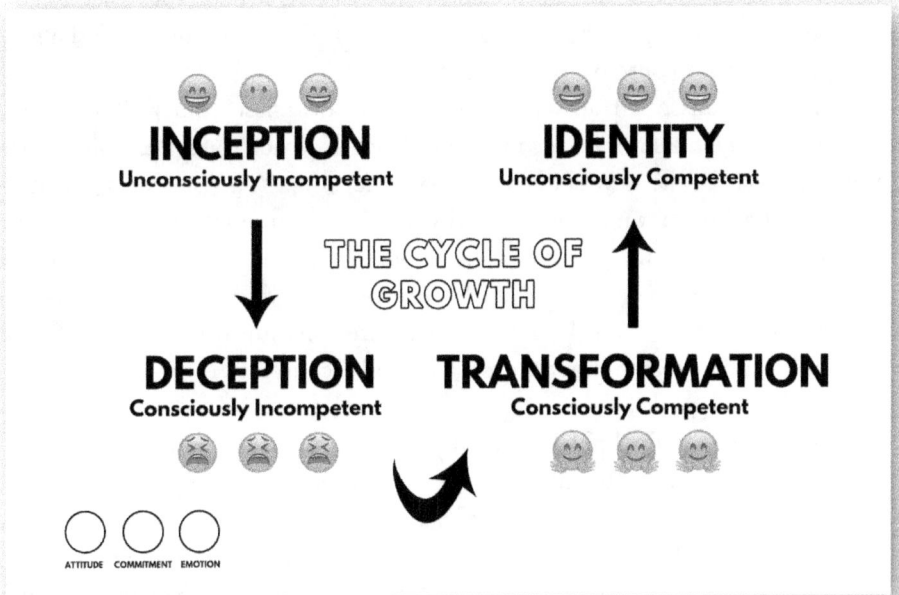

INCEPTION
Unconsciously Incompetent

IDENTITY
Unconsciously Competent

THE CYCLE OF GROWTH

DECEPTION
Consciously Incompetent

TRANSFORMATION
Consciously Competent

ATTITUDE   COMMITMENT   EMOTION

The first phase of the cycle of growth is called inception, and in this phase, you don't know what you don't know. What I mean by this is everything is new, so you are excited, your attitude is at a high positive level, and your commitment level is zero initially because you aren't yet completely invested since you're just getting started. You set out excitedly to make a difference, change the world, or accomplish something great, and you are happy, excited, and positive. Your emotions are high, and again in this phase you don't know what you don't know, so you are unconsciously incompetent at this point.

The second phase you will enter into is the most challenging for most people, and is called deception. Deception is when you start to learn what it is you don't yet know and start to uncover the skills you will need to acquire, learn, and refine to move forward and master your new endeavor. This is the stage where most people decide to quit, get "realistic," and fall back into their comfort zones. This is also the phase where the most growth occurs if you can push through it while learning, improving your skill set, and remaining as positive as possible. In this phase your attitude, commitment level, and emotion are all low as you push to power through to phase 3. Don't be discouraged during deception—recognize it, accept that better, more fulfilling things are coming soon, and move on and enjoy the growth process. This phase is why loving your skill, task, or mission is so vitally important. If you love it, it makes it easier to stay persistent, continue growing, and power through the deception phase. During deception you are consciously incompetent.

The third phase is transformation. During this phase your attitude, commitment level, and emotion begin to shift from low back to high as you further learn and master the new skills necessary to level up. You start seeing positive results and gaining momentum toward your goals, and more importantly, your identity begins to shift. You start to see yourself as a person who is successful and achieves what he or she sets out to achieve rather than a person who is still trying to figure things out. In this phase you are consciously competent, as you can successfully execute, but you still have to be conscious of what and how to do things, so to speak.

The fourth and final phase is when you create the new identity you've been working toward. Your attitude, commitment level, and energy are all as high as they were when you first began in inception; however, you now have developed and mastered the skills necessary to execute successfully at an unconscious level. You are now unconsciously competent, and living out your purpose at a world-class level just happens because that is who you are now. Your personal identity has completely shifted to being the person you've been dreaming, visualizing, and creating. It's not easy to get to this point and make a true identity shift, but if you love what you are doing and believe you are living your true purpose, it will help you to stay the course and infinitely raise your chances for success through positive perseverance.

You also have to be good at whatever it is because for you to take it to the level where it both serves others in a profound way and is valuable to both you and them, you're going to have to be better at it than most. This means if you work and develop something you aren't very good at, you will become better at it, but your "better" will most likely be the point where someone who is naturally good at the same thing would be starting. Instead of going from lacking to proficient or average, you want to go from good to great or even world-class. You will serve more people and yourself at a much higher level by focusing on and leveling up your natural strengths and not paying attention to your weaknesses.

We all have weaknesses, and the key is not to fall in love with them. Society tells us to practice what we aren't good at and has us buying into the idea that we can become better at those things and make a difference. What is actually happening is we are creating a world full of people who are average at everything instead a world full of people who are world-class at certain things. If you aren't good at something, don't fret. Team up with someone else who is naturally good at what you're not. Allow that person to shine there and you to shine where you're meant to shine. LeBron isn't spending the entire off-season taking batting practice because he's trying to shore up his weakness—he's putting in the time making his already naturally ridiculous skill at basketball even better and more developed. Be your own LeBron in what you're good at, and keep shooting your own version of free throws until you can't miss. Embrace your natural strengths and skills; the world needs them.

The next important point and purpose question is about using what you love and are good at to serve others, and that is another vital piece. The people who serve the most get paid the most, and getting paid is important and something we will talk about in a minute. LeBron gets paid more than most people because his skill set is so rare, refined, and developed that it makes him world-class at playing basketball. When people say pro athletes are overpaid and complain about their contracts, it makes my blood boil.

Everyone has the exact same opportunities as human beings. True, I don't have the natural abilities to become a professional basketball or baseball player, but I do have other natural abilities that are on par with pro athletes in other areas. Pro athletes don't come out of the womb with huge contracts to play in front of millions of people. They practice, train, work hard, and develop their natural skills to the point where they are the best in the world at what they do. They serve millions of people by providing an entire subculture of entertainment, fashion, and competitiveness. They also give up things people who aren't professional athletes or celebrities take for granted, like going out to a normal peaceful family dinner or a movie unbothered.

My point is instead of complaining about their success, be grateful they are the embodiment of what's "realistic" when you find what you are naturally good at, love it enough to develop it to the point of world-class, and then use it to serve as many people as possible. They are living their purposes at an extremely high level and are successful because of it—they deserve all the money they are paid. You want to make pro athlete–type money? Follow the success theory, become one of the best in the world at something you are naturally good at and love doing, and use it to serve as many people as pro athletes do, and you too will be compensated accordingly.

Finally, let's chat about getting paid. Money is a vital tool for anyone who desires to make a positive difference in the world. Whether that difference is purely for you and your family or maybe to give back to those less fortunate who don't have the same opportunities to create success in their lives as you do, the fact of the matter is you can't give what you don't have. Not having money serves absolutely nobody, while having money gives you the opportunity to serve a lot of people.

Everyone has his or her own feelings when it comes to money, but money is nothing more than a tool. Just as a hammer is to a carpenter, money is to everyone. Money is simply something we trade for something else. You go to the grocery store and trade money for food; you go to the mall and trade money for clothes; you pay your mortgage and trade money for shelter. Money is a tool we use for trade, and the more value you can provide to others, the more money they will trade you to provide that value. It's much like when you buy tickets to watch your favorite sports team or to see your favorite artist or band in concert; you trade money for the opportunity to be entertained for a few hours by people who have developed their natural abilities to a world-class level.

When you do something better than most and you use it to serve others in a positive manner, there is absolutely nothing wrong with being paid for doing it. In fact, there is far more wrong with not being paid. For you to effectively give your mastered talents to the world, you have to receive something in return. Anytime something is given, something must also be received. It's a universal law, and it's actually the second universal law of success. The law of giving and receiving is based on the fact that everything in the universe operates through dynamic exchange. Giving and receiving are different aspects of the flow of energy in the universe. **It isn't better to give than to receive; they are equally important.** Learn to be good at and happy with both giving and receiving, for they are both vital to creating your own success.

In the next section, we will talk about strategic planning, refining, and mastery when it comes to the success theory. Action is where the magic happens, and we are going to get into all that as soon as you are done with the answers to the following questions.

Creating Your Success

A. What are three things you are really good at?
B. What are three ways you can use each of these things to serve others?
C. What are three things you absolutely love to do?
D. What are three ways you can use each of these things to serve others?
E. Be creative and tap into your imagination and come up with three fun ideas or projects that combine something you are good at with something you love to do, and then explain how you can use that idea/project to positively affect and serve others.
F. Reread your answer to question E in section I, and now recreate your perfect day using the framework you already created while incorporating one of your fun ideas/projects from your answer to question E in section II.

SECTION III

Strategic Planning, Refining, and Mastery

B y this point you should at least have your wheels spinning. You should be really thinking about your purpose and how your personal talents, skills, and desires fit together to help you work toward fulfilling your purpose at a high level and, conversely, creating your own vision of success in your life.

One point I'd like to make before diving into planning and mastery is success is actually a consequence of fulfilling your purpose at a high level. While it's very important to know what your vision of success looks and feels like, it's also very important that you don't strive merely to create that image in your life. It sounds counterintuitive, but once you understand these principles to the point where you intuitively feel them at your core, it will make perfect sense.

It's vital to know and feel what your vision of success looks like so the universe and circumstance begin to attract it to you, but it's not your place to try to take control and jump right to the end from the beginning. To create your success vision and make it real in your life, you need to focus on fulfilling your purpose using the skills or things you both love and are good at. If you focus on, master, and do this, your success vision will come to fruition and be your reality as a consequence. Know and feel the end result you desire to create, and all the while focus on living out your purpose at the highest level you possibly can—that's the game, and that's how you will have sustainable, fulfilling success in your life according to your own vision.

It's incredibly vital you understand, buy into, and accept what I just explained with every fiber of your being before moving on to strategic planning, refining, and mastery. By the way, those three phrases are just a fancy way of saying to take educated, massive action while constantly aiming to improve until you become the best you possibly can be at your craft.

The reason you need to make the process your purpose is because if you are focused on the wrong things, you will take the wrong actions, and if you are constantly practicing the wrong actions, you will get really good at doing the wrong things. Being really good at doing the wrong things is like LeBron batting in the bottom of the ninth in game 7 of the World Series with two outs and the tying run on third. The best basketball player in the world has the entire baseball season on his shoulders, and believe me: as exceptional an athlete as LeBron is, that game is not going to end well for his team. It's not LeBron's fault; he's just been practicing and playing basketball his entire life and in this scenario is expected to perform in the game of baseball at the highest level in the world. Do you see my point? You don't want to be LeBron at the dish; you want to be LeBron at the free throw line.

I'm sure at least once in your life you've heard the famous saying "Practice makes perfect." Well, I'm here to tell you it's complete nonsense! Practice doesn't make perfect—perfect practice makes perfect. What's the point of practicing if you're getting good at the wrong things? The point here is to focus on the process so you know exactly what you are trying to achieve and also have a great barometer of how much you are improving.

While all this is important stuff, perhaps the most important thing to consider is taking action. Most people spend all their time getting ready to get ready. They believe they need to read one more book or take one more course or listen to one more podcast to get the secret thing they have been missing. While consumption and constantly growing as a person and learning are vitally important, without action it never comes to fruition. Growth is only half of the fulfillment equation we talked about earlier in this book. The other half is contribution, and you can't contribute effectively unless you are taking action.

It's important that you take some form of action IMMEDIATELY. By that I mean right now, this very second. Do something that's going to get momentum started in your direction. The entire process of practicing and mastering a task is predicated on creating momentum. Without momentum you will always be at the same point you are now, which is the starting point of success. Once you get into action, momentum begins to be created, and taking strategic educated action while improving a little each time eventually leads to mastery—and once you've mastered your craft and serve more people at a higher level than anyone else, you will be on a world-class level.

Most people believe they have to be "motivated" before they can take effective action, and I'm here to tell you not only is this a false assumption but it's flat out backward. Motivation is something you create with momentum, not something that causes you to take action. Motivation is something I see people in today's meme/quote-heavy world using as an excuse rather than what it really is.

As long as you're busy getting motivated and feeling all the feels that come along with that, you don't have to take action—well, to get results you do, but again, who needs results when you can get the feeling from a motivational quote, sound bite, video, or book? Motivation is becoming a drug in the success world, as it gives you great feelings, almost a high, without doing anything. The problem is these feelings last only a short time and will never yield anything substantial, as they serve only one person instead of the masses. As you know, service is the third part of the success theory, and that makes it a major, major part of success.

I like progression and visualization, as to me they make things more real. That's why I love to use a dry-erase board when I'm brainstorming. To make this concept about motivation more visual, allow me to explain it this way:

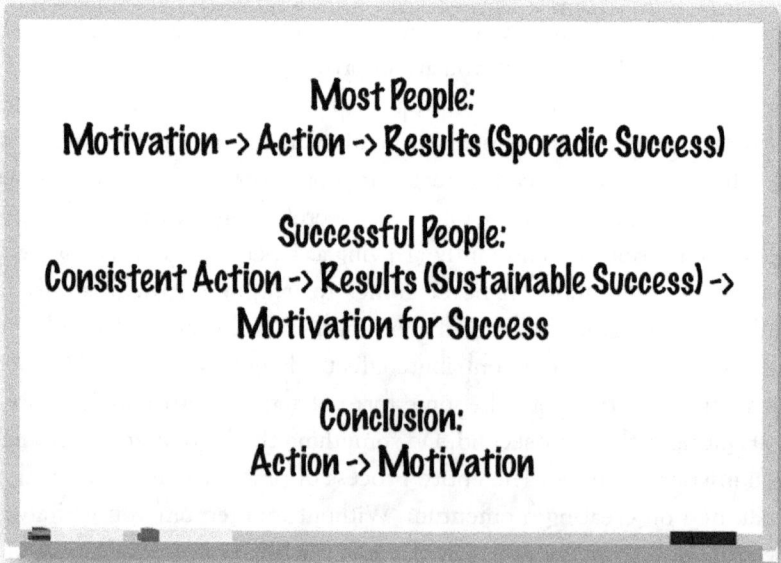

Most People:
Motivation -> Action -> Results (Sporadic Success)

Successful People:
Consistent Action -> Results (Sustainable Success) -> Motivation for Success

Conclusion:
Action -> Motivation

As you can see, most of us think about it completely backward. Motivation doesn't lead to success; success actually leads to motivation, which in turn leads to more action, which ultimately leads to more results or success. **Stop trying to be so motivated, and start doing things that make you a motivating person to others.**

Now, I should say you don't necessarily have to reach the world-class level to be successful; it's up to you to decide what level equates to your personal success vision. One thing I do know, though, is goals change over time, especially once they are achieved. As human beings, we are always aiming for that next level. Today you want to get that promotion, but then what? You don't have to answer that question right this second, but just realize this, and plan to go further than you think you want to go today.

As human beings we often underestimate what we can accomplish and what we are capable of—remember that if it's available for the world, it's also available for you; it's just a matter of how. And the "how" is through constant action and improvement that leads to mastery.

Not everyone does or has to aspire to being successful or reaching his or her personal success vision, but the fact that you are reading this handbook and putting in the work to figure things out for yourself tells me you have that burning desire and ambition to go further and achieve more. That fact in itself is something you should be celebrating every day as you go over your success vision in your mind's eye.

Right now, though, let's talk about strategic planning. Strategic planning is having an idea of the actions you should be taking or you'd like to try to take. I like to do my planning immediately after seeing and feeling my success vision through visualization. I find that my vibration, belief, energy, and enthusiasm are at their peak right then, and this puts me in the most resourceful and creative state to be planning. Creativity is key for this process; you can be only as creative as the state you are in at the moment. Remember that achieving your success vision has very little to do with your actual resources and everything to do with your resourcefulness at any given time—creativity and action are invaluable.

I like to practice my visualization first thing in the morning so it's fresh to start my day. As soon as I finish, I make a list of three actions I can accomplish today to take me closer to making my vision a reality. I then take immediate action and accomplish at least one, if not all three, of these items, and I celebrate to myself as I accomplish them. Some of these action items are the same things each day; they are actions I am mastering and getting better at each time I execute them. Some of them are new ideas I want to try to see how they work. In any case, I craft and execute them with my outcome in mind but with the goal of living my life's purpose to the absolute best of my abilities at that moment.

Strategic planning is the ability to take into account all the previous actions you have taken and use that experience with your creativity in peak state to create a fresh list of action items that fulfill your life's purpose while consequently creating your personal success vision. Like every skill in life and the actions we've already discussed, strategic planning gets easier the more you take action and practice it.

Refinement is also crucial and is part of the above process. Refinement is the ability to learn what is serving you and others and what isn't and then be able to do more of what is and less of what isn't in a more efficient way each and every day. It's not enough to practice and become purely more skilled; you have to become more efficient at the same time. This means you are not only becoming better at executing but you can also execute more of the things that serve both you and others at the same time. The most successful people not only serve people at a world-class level but also serve more people at this level. Refining your skills and becoming more efficient through repetition is a major key to the success theory and manifesting your personal success vision.

Mastery is simply the ability to do what you do at an extremely high level as efficiently as possible. The most popular explanation of mastery comes from Malcolm Gladwell's fantastic book *Outliers*, where he tells us that it takes, on average, ten thousand hours of practice to master any skill. Whether the number is ten thousand or fourteen thousand or twenty thousand is irrelevant; the point is that mastery takes time, effort, persistence, practice, and the desire to constantly improve.

Mastery is a major piece to the success theory, and mastery is the main reason why you must both love and be good at what you are pursuing. Mastery takes commitment and dedication, and it's hard to have either of those things, let alone both, to something you don't particularly like. You have to love what you are doing so you can master it and continue working toward it through not only inevitable setbacks but also the negativity and tests the outside world will throw at you. Your resolve will be tested, but the good news is once you prove yourself to the universe, it will turn around and serve you in more ways than you can fathom. The problem is most people never get to that point because they don't absolutely love what they are doing, so they give up prematurely.

The other aspect we discussed previously is you have to be naturally good at whatever you are focusing on pursuing. Again, mastery is an extremely high level of execution, so you need to have that base of being somewhat skilled in whatever arena you are in. There's always something to be said for natural talent, and it is an invaluable resource; however, talent that is not practiced and refined will always be just good. With desire, lack of talent that is practiced and refined can become great, but talent that is practiced and refined over time becomes world-class. You cannot become world-class without talent. You can achieve greatness, but even that takes an extraordinary amount of effort. Most people who insist on pursuing an area where they lack talent end up being very good at what they do, but to be world-class, you have to start with talent and then practice and refine that talent day in and day out.

Talent and action are the variables. Effective practice and refinement can be done by anyone with strategic planning and desire; however, true mastery and world-class results come from talent mixed with loving what you do, planning strategically, refining both your skill set and approach, and then using that heavily refined and specialized skill set to efficiently serve as many people as possible. If you do serve your true purpose by doing what I just described, you will have no choice but to manifest your success vision as a consequence.

Service is the next piece of the equation, and every piece is just as important as the last. Answer the following questions so you can start brainstorming and creating ideas and action items toward mastery in your own life.

Let me just say you don't have to stop whatever it is you do now to pursue your true purpose. Maybe you are already pursuing your purpose; you just need a fresh approach to maximize your results and put you on track to serving more people at a higher level. Or maybe you need a fresh approach in some area of your life to create true feelings of fulfillment for yourself. In any case, doing these exercises and answering the questions at the end of each section is a great way to open your mind, explore, and get creative.

Happiness is the true goal we are all searching for—living a life full of happiness while paying it forward and helping others do the same. Working on yourself and practicing and refining your talents even part time is a great way to start the beautiful snowball of momentum. Get into constructive action, and start making things happen as much as you possibly can today, even if it is just a small action and a small step. Small steps lead to big results over time, and positive energy and results create and attract more positive energy and results. What I'm trying to say is doing something is ALWAYS better than doing nothing, and I'm equally proud of you and excited for you to be taking this journey and trusting me to be your guide as we move on to the section about serving the world.

Creating Your Success

A. What excites you the most about your perfect day as you described it in answer F of section II?

B. Create a list of twelve action items you can realistically accomplish within the next ten days that will begin to create momentum toward executing your new idea/project, and again, be as descriptive as possible.

C. What are three daily actions you can complete and use to create consistency toward honing the skills necessary to execute your new exciting idea/project?

D. Whom can you share your idea, vision, and daily method of operation (DMO) you described in answer C of section III with that you can count on to support you, push you, and hold you accountable?

E. What are you willing to give up or commit to in order to create a "no-fail environment" for yourself?

F. How many hours per day are you going to commit to practice toward mastering your craft?

G. Refer to the answer to question F of section III, and calculate the amount of time it will take you to reach ten thousand hours of practice.

Serving the World

Imagine the people who are or were considered the best in the world at what they do. George Washington, Benjamin Franklin, Thomas Jefferson, John F. Kennedy, Marilyn Monroe, Elvis Presley, Albert Einstein, Michael Jordan, Roberto Clemente, the Beatles, Billy Joel, Michael Jackson, Steve Jobs, Bill Gates, Beyoncé, LeBron James, Lady Gaga, Bruno Mars, Dwayne "the Rock" Johnson, and there are so many more—but these are the ones who come to my mind initially. How amazing is the talent pool, and how much mastery did they each put into their crafts? It's really mind blowing how much these people have changed the world and how much they all created in their lives.

Now, imagine these people still existed with the same level of talent and the same level of mastery in their lives, BUT they never left their parents' basements. Not that there's anything wrong with living in the basement, but what if that level of talent and mastery never came out to see the light of day and share what they had to offer? The world as we know it would be dramatically different, and the lives they live also would be dramatically different.

A classic philosophical question asks, if a tree falls in the forest and no one is around to hear it, does it make a sound? It's a thought experiment that challenges observation and knowledge of reality. Let's dive into this question a bit further, not because the actual answer has anything to do with serving the world, but because the type of thinking it requires to dissect this conundrum is the same type of thinking that will lead us to see how vital service is to the success theory and manifesting your personal success vision.

First, let's consider what sound really is—vibrations that travel through the air or another medium and can be heard when they reach a person's or animal's ear. Sound is an experience, and it's hard to explain to another person, but now that you know the definition and what it really consists of, you should be well equipped. In any case, sound is simply vibrations that travel through the air, making the real question, does there have to be a person or animal present with functioning ears to process, decode, and actually hear that sound? My personal answer to this question is absolutely! If a tree falls and no one is there to allow the sound to enter the ear canal, all that is really produced is a bunch of vibrations that travel through the air until they dissipate.

So this raises a similar question that is back to our original topic: If someone finds something he or she loves and is really good at, strategically plans, practices, refines, and masters whatever this is, and then never takes it anywhere else to serve anyone else, will the person ever be successful? It's really a loaded question, because the person could be successful in other areas of life, but as for this specific area we are speaking of, I'd have to say the answer is a resounding NO!

You can do all the work up to this point, but if you don't use what you know or have to serve the world, it really does nothing but feed your ego. A famous quote states, "Knowledge unused is ignorance." At the same time, I truly believe that mastery unshared is selfish.

If you desire more in life—whether it be more money, more happiness, more love, more experiences, or more anything—you first have to share what you already have with others. If you have a jar filled to the brim, nearly overflowing, with salt but you want sugar, you first have to find someone else who has a jar full of sugar and needs salt. Then and only then can you free up some space in your own jar by sharing some of your salt with the other person, and then the person can do the same in return. It's the universal law of giving and receiving we spoke about earlier in this book.

If you want to receive anything in life, you must first give something, since giving and receiving operate through dynamic exchange. You can never give nothing and receive something, and if you do, it's only a matter of time before the universe takes something back to even things out.

The prime example of this is people who win the lottery. A lot of people who don't understand the success theory principles yearn to win the lottery. They hedge their entire futures on magically "winning" what they consider a huge, life-changing lump sum of cash. Most people spend their entire lives spending their hard-earned money to try to get lucky and win the lottery. Of course, there is no such thing as luck, but they don't understand this principle either.

Luck is merely when opportunity and preparation come together. This happens when you've been working to master your purpose and then you get the opportunity to share it with a large number of people at once—but you know it's not luck, because you've been working so hard for it for so long, even if they haven't seen it.

Back to the example, IF (and that's a big if) these people win the lottery, they are so excited and believe they deserve the amazing gift. Since they gave nothing to create this gift, other than a few dollars, it's only a matter of time before they owe just as much in some other area of their lives. Usually, within six months they are right back to the original financial position they were in before winning the lottery. They didn't go through the process and become the type of person who can create that kind of wealth. They didn't make their deposits in desire, practice, refining, mastery, and service.

The universe will help you—in fact, the universe wants to help you more than you'll ever know—but the universe can't help you until you first put in the effort and the energy to help others. It's amazing how good it feels to give to others, and there's a good reason for that.

Growth and contribution are the two key pieces to fulfillment. We are either growing or dying; there's no in-between. So it's critical to focus each and every day on growing and becoming more. The sole purpose of growing, becoming more, and having more is so you can help other people do the same. When you do this, the universe will step in and say, "Hey! You're fulfilling your purpose and serving others; now let me fulfill mine and serve you in ways only I can do."

There is a reason we spent the first three sections of this book talking about, thinking about, and discovering how to grow in a purposeful and meaningful way and are taking only one section to talk about contributing what you've become. The reason is contributing is generally an organic part of growth. When you are passionately living your purpose and growing and mastering what you are meant to, it's nearly impossible not to be contributing to others along the way. The idea, though, is to take the organic part of that process and make it intentional.

As you are growing and developing, you should be constantly thinking about these questions:

How can I serve others more?
How can I serve others better?
How can I can serve more people in a
more efficient and better way?

By keeping those questions front and center in your mind, you will constantly be growing with the intent to serve, which is infinitely more powerful than growing to grow and then worrying about serving later.

The success theory is a process or equation in which one part leads to the next in order to lead to the next to create a systematic result—it's synergistic.

Synergistic: relating to the interaction or cooperation of two or more organizations, substances, or other agents to produce a combined effect greater than the sum of their separate effects.

Discovering and living your purpose is important, but having a strategic plan and refining your purpose to the point of mastery makes it infinitely more important and powerful. Taking your infinitely more powerful mastered purpose to the world and using it to serve others to the absolute best of your ability will take your life and every life you touch along the way to a higher level than you knew existed.

You should always be serving people, from the beginning of the process on. Initially it won't be as dramatic or powerful an experience; it might even be a bit painful and feel extremely awkward, only because you haven't mastered or practiced the skills necessary to serve at a higher level—YET.

Growth isn't easy; in fact, it can be downright painful at times. That's why we went through the process of actually feeling the feelings of your success vision before diving into figuring out what the actions are and how to execute them. The feelings you desire and continue to visualize and feel along the way will give you the initial juice and energy, so to speak, to get through the growing pains. Once you get through those growing pains, the feelings you create from serving others through your purpose will be all the juice you need to keep going. However, it is still important to keep your personal success vision front and center in your mind and to continue visiting it regularly. The more time you spend there, the more detail you give it, and the more real you make it feel, the more powerful it will be. It will put you into that state of desire/ creative resourcefulness with the objective to serve others at the highest level. Strategic planning from this state will give you thoughts, ideas, and energy you will never find anywhere else. Serve the world and others from this place with this desire, and the universe will reciprocate and compensate you by making your success vision a reality and manifesting that life for you to grow into and live every single day.

It's not easy, and it shouldn't be, because it's a place and a course of action very few are willing to take. *Are you willing to let go of everything you know and some of the things you already have to make room for the things you really want?* That's the real question, and that's where the desire for real action is born.

I think the best overall guide to life that I've ever seen and that can absolutely be tied into the success theory is found in the Prayer of Saint Francis. No matter what you believe spiritually, there is a ton of wisdom to be found in his words. If you are spiritual, this is a great prayer to incorporate into your life. I especially like to use it just before I do my visualization, as it helps put me in my desired state before feeling my personal feelings of success through growth and contribution.

Saint Francis is a perfect example and study for the success theory. Saint Francis was the son of a prosperous silk merchant and lived a comfortable childhood with many friends. Eventually he felt God calling him, and he cast aside his wealth and inheritance and lived in poverty, caring for the poor and the sick while trusting in God to provide for him day to day. Now, there are a ton of other very interesting details to learn about the life of Saint Francis of Assisi, and I recommend doing some research and learning more about his life, the decisions he made, and his overall path.

The important thing to understand about the life of Saint Francis in regard to the success theory is he could have lived a "normal" life by receiving his inheritance and just being comfortable. However, he felt a bigger calling or purpose for his life, and he pursued it wholeheartedly. It absolutely wasn't easy, but as Saint Francis grew and became more loving, compassionate, and wise, he shared these gifts with others. He took care of the poor, cared for animals, spread the message of God, and started the Franciscan friars, which are still around. He served so much that he became a saint and even had a pope take his name. And I can almost guarantee that even though his life was extremely difficult at times, it was also equally fulfilling to live out his purpose at that level and serve so many.

Now, we are not all going to be saints, and we are not all called to do the same things. We each have a unique purpose in life, but studying the lives of other great people who lived their purposes and mastered the success theory can give us insight and wisdom as it relates to our own journeys. You don't have to be Catholic or even religious to respect and be in awe of someone who gives up everything he or she has to be able to grasp something he or she is passionate about and, in doing so, positively affect the lives of so many for years to come. I think it's safe to say Saint Francis will continue to have a lasting impact on the world and on human beings for as long as we can fathom. You don't have to take it that far in your own life, but I always get joy, hope, excitement, and happiness out of seeing what is possible in the world.

Prayer of Saint Francis

Lord, make me an instrument of Your peace. Where there is hatred, let me sow love; where there is injury, pardon; where there is doubt, faith; where there is despair, hope; where there is darkness, light; where there is sadness, joy.

O, Divine Master, grant that I may not so much seek to be consoled as to console; to be understood as to understand; to be loved as to love; For it is in giving that we receive; it is in pardoning that we are pardoned; it is in dying that we are born again to eternal life.

So what's next? Excellent question. The next step is continuous and never-ending improvement, and the best way I know how to do that is working with an accountability partner, mastermind group, or coach. In the next section, we will discuss all these options and more to help you create the results you desire so you manifest, live, and serve while you live out your purpose and personal success vision.

Creating Your Success

A. Using the answers you've already created, how many people would you like to serve with your new idea/project over the course of your first year?

B. Who is your ideal client/audience? Create an avatar by creating a person/people and then naming them and describing their lives in as much detail as possible.

C. If you were going to run into your ideal client/audience randomly in the morning, afternoon, and evening, where would you run into them? Where are they spending their time?

D. If you were going to plan three separate outings with your ideal client/audience, where would you plan to go?

E. List ten fun and creative ways you can get your new idea/project in front of as many people as possible.

F. List ten fun and creative ways you can get your new idea/project in front of your ideal client/audience.

Putting It All Together

The success theory, just like many things in life, is extremely simple. It's easy to understand and figure out, but at the same time, it can be extremely difficult to execute. What makes it tough is you have to break through your own clutter, limiting beliefs, and comfort zones, as well as the opinions and thoughts of others, to fight the status quo and rise up on the other side a new person living a new dream.

When you're reading this handbook and doing the exercises, it gets really exciting! I mean, we as humans were built to dream and make a difference in the world. It feels good to visualize that and put yourself there for even a few minutes. But then comes the time to roll up your sleeves and put in the work, because for these dreams to manifest, real work has to be done and momentum has to be built.

I'm not here to give you a rah-rah speech at the conclusion of this handbook to motivate you and make you feel good about yourself. That's not what I'm here for, and that's not why I wrote this book and have the intense desire to share my ideas with the world to make it a better place. The truth is either you're ready or you're not, and nothing I say is going to change that. I want to help anyone who is looking for my help, and for me to do that, you have to dig down deep within yourself and figure out whether you're ready to give it all you've got to potentially create everything you want. You have to be ready, because I've said it before and I'll say it again—nothing changes if nothing changes. You have to step up and be ready.

If you're open, motivated, driven, inspired, and coachable and have a deep desire to grow as a person, discover your purpose, put in the effort to master that purpose, and use it to serve as many people as possible, then we need to take this conversation a step further. This handbook highlights the fundamentals of creating the success vision you personally desire to live out. You can keep coming back to this book time and time again for guidance and the questions and exercises that will help you get onto the path you desire to be on. This is a great start, but it is just that—a start.

If you want to take things further, you need to go a bit further. Now that you have that solid foundation forming, the best thing you can do for yourself is find a mentor who can both hold you accountable and push you further so you achieve and accomplish more. You'll also want to hook up with a group of positive-thinking, like-minded people.

First, a mentor or coach is extremely important because he or she generally has experiences you don't and, at the same time, cares about you and wants you to succeed. More importantly though, he or she is an extra set of eyes that aren't as close to your life and situation as you are.

Let's do a quick exercise. Take this book, press the page you are reading up against your nose, and continue reading. Now that you're back, hold the book where you can comfortably read the text, and ask yourself why you couldn't read it when it was pressed up against your nose. I'm sure you've figured out it's because your face was so close to the page you couldn't see the entire thing. Life is exactly the same way. When we are in it and as close to our circumstances, stories, and everyday occurrences as we are, we can't see the entire picture. However, a coach or mentor not only is able to see and observe more but is usually able to do it with a wiser, more experienced eye. We all need a mentor, and I personally have a few of them I work with.

The other thing to remember is you are the sum of the five people you spend the most time with. If you are the smartest person in your circle of friends, then it's probably time to find some new friends to start hanging around. I'm not saying get rid of the friends you have; I'm just saying if you really want to grow, you should spend more time with people who challenge you and force you to grow.

That's also the reason you want to find a group of like-minded people to regularly associate with. Unfortunately, the world can tend to be a bit of a negative place—especially if you are trying to grow and create more and the people who are regularly in your life aren't. Again, you can still spend some time with them, but spending a majority of your time there will tend to cause their negative energy to rub off on you, and that only makes growth and development even more difficult a task. When you have a group of positive-thinking, like-minded people who support you, push you toward success, help you to grow, encourage you regularly, allow you to contribute value to them in return, and recharge your success batteries, so to speak, it is invaluable.

We all need help and support, as true growth cannot be achieved alone. You can read all the books, listen to all the podcasts, and watch all the videos you want—but if you never get out in it with other people, exchanging ideas, encouragement, energy, and value, you will never really grow—and you certainly will never contribute to and serve others.

Throughout this book, it has been my aim to serve you by sharing value through my experiences, thoughts, and insights when it comes to creating the life you want to lead through living your true purpose, building a legacy, and serving others. The goal was to provide you some valuable information immediately followed by questions that would guide you in applying what you learned or discovered to your own life while crafting your personal success vision and then taking some form of action to begin creating momentum.

I want us to acknowledge that this book is only the beginning of your journey and, hopefully, the beginning of our journey together. I would like to offer you a very special invitation to visit us at **TheSuccessTheory.com** and check out all the different ways we can team up! From our Stir the Pot Mastermind Group to one-on-one mentoring/coaching sessions with me and/or Erica, we are always searching for new, fun, and valuable ways to serve you and help you grow.

Also keep your eyes open for our invitation-only inner-circle group called Badass in Action. We are extremely proud of this group, which spends an entire year working hands-on with us as well as one another to put the success theory into action and create their success visions, which we aptly call a Badass Life. We all put a large amount of time and energy into this elite group. It's so elite that we open only fifteen seats per year, and the value exchanged is unlike anything else we offer. Again, to be invited to join this group, which is open only once per year, you must first be a member of our Stir the Pot Mastermind Group, submit an application to show your interest, and go through the interview process. We want to work with and exchange energy with individuals who are hungry to create the lives they truly want to live. It's an amazing experience and one in which you will not only begin creating your Badass Life but also meet people and create relationships that will last a lifetime. Talk about a true one-of-a-kind opportunity to grow and contribute with a group of positive-thinking, like-minded people!

We value your thoughts, ideas, and feedback, as I truly believe we all have value to share and we can all learn from one another. Feel free to e-mail me directly at **mario@abadasslife.com** to say hi, let me know what you're thinking, and let me know how I can help you. Please e-mail Erica as well at **erica@ abadasslife.com**, as she is one of the best in the business at helping others effectively dream, create their own success visions, and summon the courage to take action and make things happen like a true Badass!

Connect with us via Facebook as well, if you haven't already, at **Facebook. com/BadassLife**. We're constantly posting and engaging and love meeting new people on that page.

If you gave me permission to make a recommendation (let's assume you did), I would tell you to complete all the questions in this handbook in as much detail as possible, visit **TheSuccessTheory.com**, join our Stir the Pot Mastermind Group, and then immediately send me an e-mail to let me know "I'M IN" so we can schedule your first one-on-one call and get momentum building for you as quickly as possible.

Thank you for being open enough to take the journey through this book with us. We look forward to meeting you and serving you in the very near future—whether online, at an event, or in person.

Our mission, as always, is to help you do life a better way…YOUR way!

Section I: Redefining Success
Creating Your Success Questions

A. What does success look like to you?

B. What are three specific areas of your life where you consider yourself successful?

C. Where would you like to create more success in your life, and what does that look like? Be as descriptive as possible.

D. Who is the most successful person you know personally, and what are three questions you would like to ask this person about his or her success?

E. If you could wake up tomorrow and live as if time and money were no issue in your life, in detail, what exactly would your day look like?

Notes and Reflections

Section II: Talent and Purpose
There are four questions you need to ask yourself to uncover your true purpose:

1. What do I love to do?

2. What am I naturally good at?

3. How can I combine these things in a manner that will serve others?

4. How can I use this to serve as many people as possible and get paid to do that?

Creating Your Success Questions

A. What are three things you are really good at?

B. What are three ways you can use each of these things to serve others?

C. What are three things you absolutely love to do?

D. What are three ways you can use each of these things to serve others?

E. Be creative and tap into your imagination and come up with three fun ideas or projects that combine something you are good at with something you love to do, and then explain how you can use that idea/project to positively affect and serve others.

F. Reread your answer to question E in section I, and now recreate your perfect day using the framework you already created while incorporating one of your fun ideas/projects from your answer to question E in section II.

Notes and Reflections

Section III: Strategic Planning, Refining, and Mastery
Creating Your Success Questions

A. What excites you the most about your perfect day as you described it in answer F of section II?

B. Create a list of twelve action items you can realistically accomplish within the next ten days that will begin to create momentum toward executing your new idea/project, and again, be as descriptive as possible.

C. What are three daily actions you can complete and use to create consistency toward honing the skills necessary to execute your new exciting idea/project?

D. Whom can you share your idea, vision, and daily method of operation (DMO) you described in answer C of section III with that you can count on to support you, push you, and hold you accountable?

E. What are you willing to give up or commit to in order to create a "no-fail environment" for yourself?

F. How many hours per day are you going to commit to practice toward mastering your craft?

G. Refer to the answer to question F of section III, and calculate the amount of time it will take you to reach ten thousand hours of practice.

Notes and Reflections

Section IV: Serving the World
Creating Your Success Questions

A. Using the answers you've already created, how many people would you like to serve with your new idea/project over the course of your first year?

B. Who is your ideal client/audience? Create an avatar by creating a person/ people and then naming them and describing their lives in as much detail as possible.

C. If you were going to run into your ideal client/audience randomly in the morning, afternoon, and evening, where would you run into them? Where are they spending their time?

D. If you were going to plan three separate outings with your ideal client/audience, where would you plan to go?

Notes and Reflections

E-mail: **mario@abadasslife.com** or **erica@abadasslife.com**
Connect: **http://www.facebook.com/BadassLife**
Join: **http://www.thesuccesstheory.com/**—Stir the Pot Mastermind Group

About Badass Life

Badass Life is a business-based lifestyle-coaching agency committed to helping you live the life you want by creating the business you need. Cofounded by Mario Porreca and Erica Parr, Badass Life works with clients one on one and in group settings to design a badass life and the practical steps they need to get there. To continue to grow in the concepts from this book, visit http://www.abadasslife.com.

> # We empower inspired young entrepreneurs to defy the status quo by creating physical & financial freedom & helping others do the same.

About Mario Porreca

Mario Porreca is a renowned chef. He was the sous chef at the number one city club in America and winner of two gold medals in cooking competitions. Porreca has authored two cookbooks, appeared on more than fifty television shows, and hosted his own radio show for three years. He left the cooking industry to focus his attention on helping others. Porreca transformed himself from a chef to an entrepreneur in six months and used the lessons he learned to develop his success theory.

About Erica Parr

Erica Parr is Porreca's partner and author of the fore-word in *The Success Theory Handbook*. She worked in marketing and handled accounts reaching $25 million in gross annual revenue. Parr realized she needed a change as well. Porreca's success theory helped her transform her life. Now, Porreca and Parr maintain their branded Badass Life and live in Pittsburgh, Pennsylvania, with their puppy, Winston.

www.ingramcontent.com/pod-product-compliance
Lightning Source LLC
LaVergne TN
LVHW021546080426
835509LV00019B/2873